OUR FAMILY CHRISTMAS MEMORIES

**A KEEPSAKE TO CAPTURE
YOUR CHRISTMAS
TRADITIONS AND MEMORIES**

MW00647910

The
FAMILY
CHRISTMAS
MEMORIES
of

Our Family
Christmas Memories

Christmastime brings us some of our most joyful and cherished memories. Families gather, old traditions are celebrated, and new ones created. *Our Family Christmas Memories* is the perfect place to record the unique and beautiful ways that your family celebrates the season.

The book begins with Our Christmas Traditions where you can record all your family's favorite Christmas customs and practices. The main section of the book is dedicated to ten chapters for you to record the details of ten Christmases. Note who came to visit, parties you attended or hosted, who cooked Christmas dinner, and what the favorite gifts were that year. These little details, which may seem insignificant as you write them, can spark memories and stories years later as you share this book with the next generation.

As you document your Christmas celebrations through the decade, collect and record favorite family recipes in the last section of the book. Don't let secret recipes vanish into family lore! Pass them on to the next generation by including them here.

As soon as you fill in your family's name on the book plate, you begin creating a family heirloom that will be treasured for many Christmases to come.

Merry Christmas to you and yours!

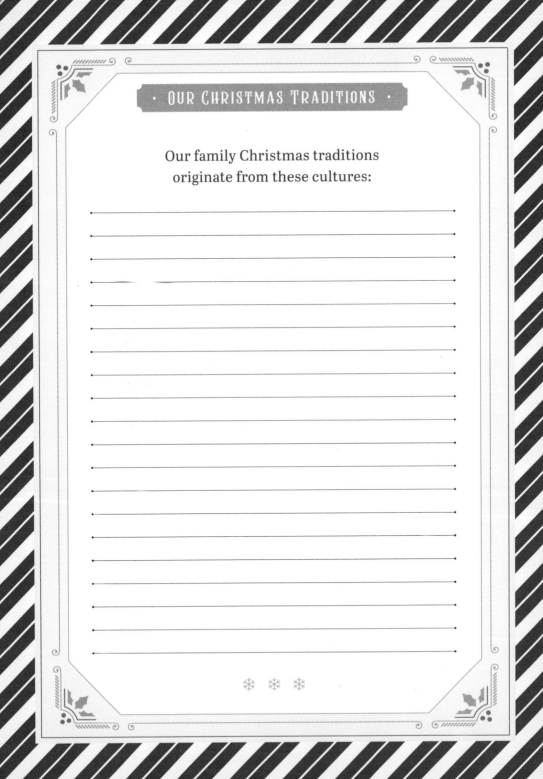

· OUR CHRISTMAS TRADITIONS ·

Our family Christmas traditions
originate from these cultures:

· OUR CHRISTMAS TRADITIONS ·

We start decorating for Christmas:

*(ex: right after Halloween, Thanksgiving weekend,
or somewhere within the 12 days of Christmas)*

_____

_____

_____

_____

_____

_____

❄ ❄ ❄

We've always decorated then because:

_____

_____

_____

_____

_____

_____

❄ ❄ ❄

· OUR CHRISTMAS TRADITIONS ·

Some of our favorite decorations are:

_____
_____
_____
_____
_____
_____
_____

❄ ❄ ❄

They're our favorites because:

_____
_____
_____
_____
_____
_____
_____

❄ ❄ ❄

· OUR CHRISTMAS TRADITIONS ·

We've always had a live/artificial
Christmas tree because:

_____

_____

_____

_____

❄   ❄   ❄

We top the tree with:

(ex: angel, star, something else)

_____

_____

❄   ❄   ❄

and this is our tradition around it:

_____

_____

_____

_____

_____

❄   ❄   ❄

· OUR CHRISTMAS TRADITIONS ·

Every year, we volunteer at or donate to:

_____

_____

_____

_____

_____

_____

_____

_____

_____

_____

_____

_____

_____

_____

_____

_____

_____

_____

_____

_____

_____

❄ ❄ ❄

· OUR CHRISTMAS TRADITIONS ·

This tradition started when:

_____
_____
_____
_____
_____
_____
_____
_____
_____
_____
_____
_____
_____
_____
_____
_____
_____
_____
_____

❄ ❄ ❄

Our advent calendar is:

(ex: homemade, filled with something fun, different every year)

❋ ❋ ❋

To see holiday lights, we:

(ex: drive around different neighborhoods, go through a drive-through lights display, look at our own house)

❋ ❋ ❋

· OUR CHRISTMAS TRADITIONS ·

This is a holiday tradition that goes way back in our family:

(ex: Feast of the Seven Fishes, putting out shoes for St. Nicholas, leaving an empty place at the table for someone who shows up unexpectedly, popping Christmas crackers)

❄ ❄ ❄

Here are a few of our favorite photos with Santa

We do/don't put out cookies and carrots for
Santa and his reindeer because:

_____
_____
_____
_____
_____
_____
_____

❄ ❄ ❄

This is what we usually leave out:

(ex: cookies, beverage, letter, "reindeer food")

_____
_____
_____
_____
_____
_____
_____

❄ ❄ ❄

· OUR CHRISTMAS TRADITIONS ·

We open presents:

*(ex: on Christmas eve, on Christmas morning, after
Christmas dinner, or some combination)*

_____

_____

_____

_____

_____

❄ ❄ ❄

This is how we typically open presents:

*(ex: one person at a time, everyone all at once, kids go first,
a certain person "plays Santa")*

_____

_____

_____

_____

_____

❄ ❄ ❄

· OUR CHRISTMAS TRADITIONS ·

Our family always watches these shows
or movies at Christmastime:

_____

_____

_____

_____

_____

_____

_____

❄ ❄ ❄

We always read this book or story:

_____

_____

_____

_____

_____

_____

_____

_____

❄ ❄ ❄

· OUR CHRISTMAS TRADITIONS ·

Our favorite Christmas carols include:

_____

_____

_____

_____

_____

_____

_____

_____

_____

_____

_____

_____

_____

_____

_____

_____

_____

_____

_____

❄   ❄   ❄

· OUR CHRISTMAS TRADITIONS ·

Some of our other family
Christmas traditions are:

_____

_____

_____

_____

_____

_____

_____

_____

_____

_____

_____

_____

_____

_____

_____

_____

_____

_____

_____

_____

❄   ❄   ❄

OUR CHRISTMAS TRADITIONS

CHRISTMAS THE YEAR OF

_____

Where we celebrated the holidays:

_____

_____

✳ ✳ ✳

How we decorated our home:

_____

_____

_____

_____

❄ ❄ ❄

This was our new ornament/decoration:

_____

_____

_____

_____

❄ ❄ ❄

New holiday experience we had this year:

_____

_____

_____

_____

❄ ❄ ❄

Christmas parties we hosted or attended:

_____

_____

_____

_____

_____

_____

_____

_____

_____

_____

_____

_____

_____

_____

_____

_____

_____

_____

_____

❄ ❄ ❄

Favorite Christmas treats
we made or enjoyed together:

_____

_____

_____

_____

_____

_____

_____

_____

_____

_____

_____

_____

_____

_____

_____

_____

_____

❄ ❄ ❄

Who was there Christmas Eve :

_____

_____

_____

_____

_____

_____

_____

_____

❄ ❄ ❄

Who was there Christmas Day :

_____

_____

_____

_____

_____

_____

_____

_____

❄ ❄ ❄

How we celebrated:

·_____
_____
·_____
·_____
·_____
·_____
·_____
·_____
·_____
·_____
·_____
·_____
·_____
·_____
·_____
·_____
·_____
·_____
·_____

❅ ❅ ❅

What we ate at our Christmas dinner and who cooked what:

_____

_____

_____

_____

_____

_____

_____

_____

_____

_____

_____

_____

_____

_____

_____

_____

_____

_____

❄   ❄   ❄

This is what we wore:

_____

_____

_____

_____

_____

_____

❄ ❄ ❄

This is who came to visit:

_____

_____

_____

_____

_____

_____

_____

❄ ❄ ❄

Memorable gifts that were exchanged and received:

_____

_____

_____

_____

_____

_____

_____

_____

_____

_____

_____

_____

_____

_____

_____

_____

_____

_____

_____

_____

❄ ❄ ❄

Favorite Christmastime
moment this year:

_____

_____

_____

_____

_____

_____

_____

_____

_____

_____

_____

_____

_____

_____

_____

_____

_____

_____

✳ ✳ ✳

This is what we are thankful for this year:

Favorite Christmas cards
we received this year:

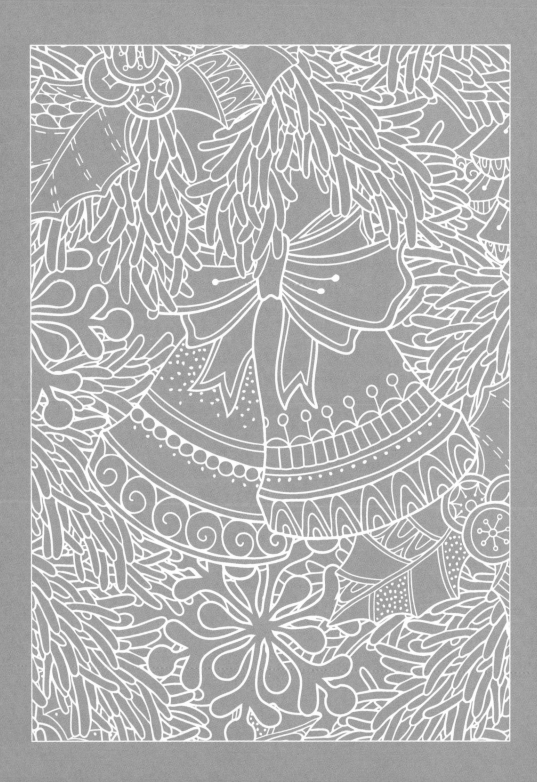

CHRISTMAS
THE
YEAR OF

_____

Where we celebrated the holidays:

_____

_____

How we decorated our home:

* * *

This was our new ornament/decoration:

* * *

New holiday experience we had this year:

* * *

Christmas parties we hosted or attended:

_____

_____

_____

_____

_____

_____

_____

_____

_____

_____

_____

_____

_____

_____

_____

_____

_____

_____

_____

❄ ❄ ❄

Favorite Christmas treats
we made or enjoyed together:

❄ ❄ ❄

Who was there Christmas Eve:

_____

_____

_____

_____

_____

_____

_____

❄ ❄ ❄

Who was there Christmas Day:

_____

_____

_____

_____

_____

_____

_____

❄ ❄ ❄

How we celebrated:

What we ate at our Christmas dinner and who cooked what:

_____

_____

_____

_____

_____

_____

_____

_____

_____

_____

_____

_____

_____

_____

_____

_____

_____

_____

_____

❄ ❄ ❄

This is what we wore:

——————————————————————
——————————————————————
——————————————————————
——————————————————————
——————————————————————
——————————————————————
——————————————————————

❄ ❄ ❄

This is who came to visit:

——————————————————————
——————————————————————
——————————————————————
——————————————————————
——————————————————————
——————————————————————
——————————————————————
——————————————————————

❄ ❄ ❄

Memorable gifts that were exchanged and received:

_____

_____

_____

_____

_____

_____

_____

_____

_____

_____

_____

_____

_____

_____

_____

_____

_____

❄ ❄ ❄

Favorite Christmastime
moment this year:

* * *

This is what we are thankful for this year:

_____

_____

_____

_____

_____

_____

_____

_____

_____

_____

_____

_____

_____

_____

_____

_____

_____

_____

❄ ❄ ❄

Favorite Christmas cards
we received this year:

CHRISTMAS
THE
YEAR OF

_____

Where we celebrated the holidays:

_____

_____

❄ ❄ ❄

How we decorated our home:

❄ ❄ ❄

This was our new ornament/decoration:

❄ ❄ ❄

New holiday experience we had this year:

❄ ❄ ❄

Christmas parties we hosted or attended:

_____

_____

_____

_____

_____

_____

_____

_____

_____

_____

_____

_____

_____

_____

_____

_____

_____

_____

_____

❄ ❄ ❄

Favorite Christmas treats
we made or enjoyed together:

_____

_____

_____

_____

_____

_____

_____

_____

_____

_____

_____

_____

_____

_____

_____

_____

_____

_____

_____

❄ ❄ ❄

Who was there Christmas Eve :

❄   ❄   ❄

Who was there Christmas Day :

❄   ❄   ❄

How we celebrated:

_____
_____
_____
_____
_____
_____
_____
_____
_____
_____
_____
_____
_____
_____
_____
_____
_____
_____
_____
_____
_____
_____

❄ ❄ ❄

What we ate at our Christmas dinner and who cooked what:

_____

_____

_____

_____

_____

_____

_____

_____

_____

_____

_____

_____

_____

_____

_____

_____

_____

_____

❄ ❄ ❄

This is what we wore:

_____

_____

_____

_____

_____

_____

_____

❄ ❄ ❄

This is who came to visit:

_____

_____

_____

_____

_____

_____

_____

_____

❄ ❄ ❄

Memorable gifts that were exchanged and received:

_____

_____

_____

_____

_____

_____

_____

_____

_____

_____

_____

_____

_____

_____

_____

_____

_____

_____

❄   ❄   ❄

Favorite Christmastime
moment this year:

_____

_____

_____

_____

_____

_____

_____

_____

_____

_____

_____

_____

_____

_____

_____

_____

_____

_____

_____

❄ ❄ ❄

This is what we are thankful for this year:

❄ ❄ ❄

Favorite Christmas cards
we received this year:

Christmas
the
Year of

_____

Where we celebrated the holidays:

_____

_____

❄ ❄ ❄

How we decorated our home:

❄ ❄ ❄

This was our new ornament/decoration:

❄ ❄ ❄

New holiday experience we had this year:

❄ ❄ ❄

Christmas parties we hosted or attended:

Favorite Christmas treats
we made or enjoyed together:

❅ ❅ ❅

Who was there Christmas Eve:

_____

_____

_____

_____

_____

_____

_____

_____

❄ ❄ ❄

Who was there Christmas Day:

_____

_____

_____

_____

_____

_____

_____

_____

❄ ❄ ❄

How we celebrated:

❄ ❄ ❄

What we ate at our Christmas dinner and who cooked what:

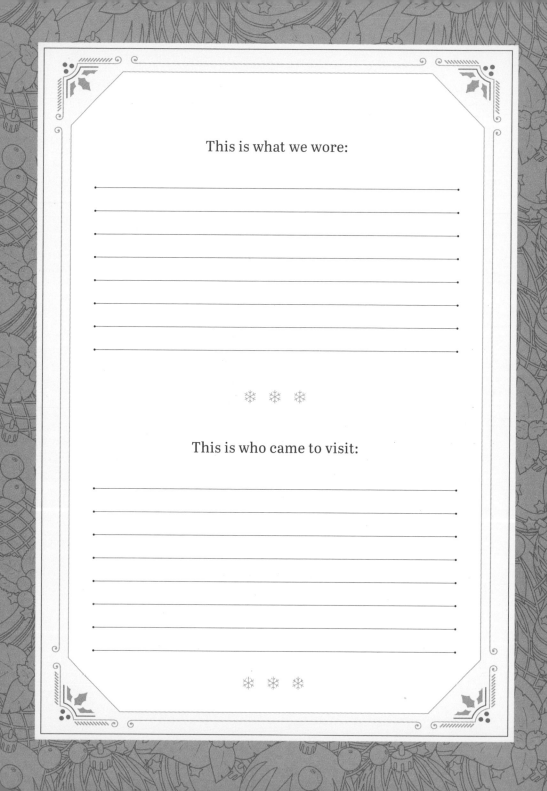

This is what we wore:

_____

_____

_____

_____

_____

_____

_____

❄ ❄ ❄

This is who came to visit:

_____

_____

_____

_____

_____

_____

_____

_____

❄ ❄ ❄

Memorable gifts that were exchanged and received:

❄ ❄ ❄

Favorite Christmastime
moment this year:

_____

_____

_____

_____

_____

_____

_____

_____

_____

_____

_____

_____

_____

_____

_____

_____

_____

_____

❄   ❄   ❄

This is what we are thankful for this year:

_____

_____

_____

_____

_____

_____

_____

_____

_____

_____

_____

_____

_____

_____

_____

_____

_____

_____

_____

❄ ❄ ❄

Favorite Christmas cards
we received this year:

Christmas the Year of

_____

Where we celebrated the holidays:

_____

_____

❄ ❄ ❄

How we decorated our home:

_____
_____
_____
_____

❄ ❄ ❄

This was our new ornament/decoration:

_____
_____
_____
_____

❄ ❄ ❄

New holiday experience we had this year:

_____
_____
_____
_____

❄ ❄ ❄

Christmas parties we hosted or attended:

❄ ❄ ❄

Favorite Christmas treats
we made or enjoyed together:

_____

_____

_____

_____

_____

_____

_____

_____

_____

_____

_____

_____

_____

_____

_____

_____

_____

_____

_____

❄   ❄   ❄

Who was there Christmas Eve :

❄   ❄   ❄

Who was there Christmas Day :

❄   ❄   ❄

How we celebrated:

What we ate at our Christmas dinner
and who cooked what:

_____

_____

_____

_____

_____

_____

_____

_____

_____

_____

_____

_____

_____

_____

_____

_____

_____

_____

_____

_____

❄   ❄   ❄

This is what we wore:

_____

_____

_____

_____

_____

_____

_____

_____

❄ ❄ ❄

This is who came to visit:

_____

_____

_____

_____

_____

_____

_____

❄ ❄ ❄

Memorable gifts that were exchanged and received:

_____

_____

_____

_____

_____

_____

_____

_____

_____

_____

_____

_____

_____

_____

_____

_____

_____

_____

❄ ❄ ❄

Favorite Christmastime
moment this year:

_____

_____

_____

_____

_____

_____

_____

_____

_____

_____

_____

_____

_____

_____

_____

_____

_____

❄ ❄ ❄

This is what we are thankful for this year:

_____

_____

_____

_____

_____

_____

_____

_____

_____

_____

_____

_____

_____

_____

_____

_____

_____

_____

_____

❋ ❋ ❋

Favorite Christmas cards
we received this year:

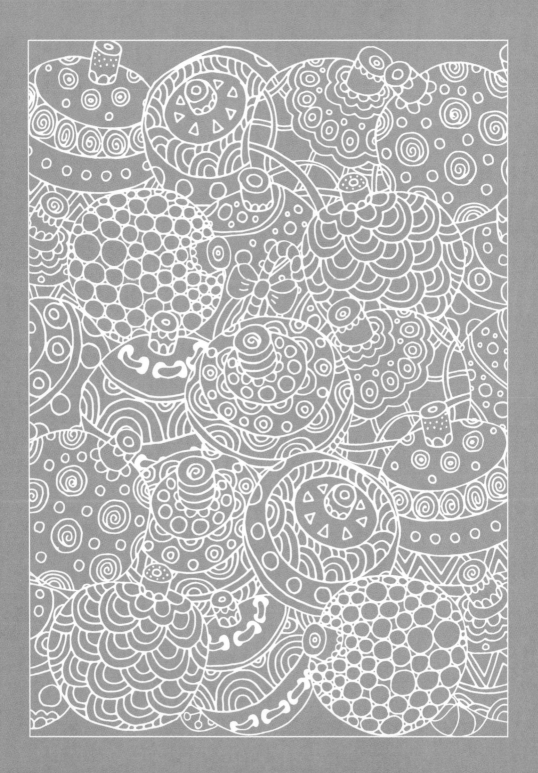

CHRISTMAS
THE
YEAR OF

_____

Where we celebrated the holidays:

_____

_____

❄ ❄ ❄

How we decorated our home:

_____

_____

_____

_____

❄ ❄ ❄

This was our new ornament/decoration:

_____

_____

_____

_____

❄ ❄ ❄

New holiday experience we had this year:

_____

_____

_____

_____

❄ ❄ ❄

Christmas parties we hosted or attended:

_____

_____

_____

_____

_____

_____

_____

_____

_____

_____

_____

_____

_____

_____

_____

_____

_____

_____

_____

❄   ❄   ❄

Favorite Christmas treats
we made or enjoyed together:

❄ ❄ ❄

Who was there Christmas Eve:

_____

_____

_____

_____

_____

_____

_____

_____

❊   ❊   ❊

Who was there Christmas Day:

_____

_____

_____

_____

_____

_____

_____

_____

❊   ❊   ❊

How we celebrated:

❄ ❄ ❄

What we ate at our Christmas dinner and who cooked what:

❄ ❄ ❄

This is what we wore:

This is who came to visit:

Memorable gifts that were
exchanged and received:

❄ ❄ ❄

Favorite Christmastime
moment this year:

_____

_____

_____

_____

_____

_____

_____

_____

_____

_____

_____

_____

_____

_____

_____

_____

_____

_____

❄   ❄   ❄

This is what we are thankful for this year:

_____
_____
_____
_____
_____
_____
_____
_____
_____
_____
_____
_____
_____
_____
_____
_____
_____
_____
_____
_____
_____
_____
_____

❄ ❄ ❄

Favorite Christmas cards
we received this year:

CHRISTMAS
THE
YEAR OF

Where we celebrated the holidays:

❄ ❄ ❄

How we decorated our home:

_____

_____

_____

_____

❄ ❄ ❄

This was our new ornament/decoration:

_____

_____

_____

_____

❄ ❄ ❄

New holiday experience we had this year:

_____

_____

_____

_____

❄ ❄ ❄

Christmas parties we hosted or attended:

❄ ❄ ❄

Favorite Christmas treats
we made or enjoyed together:

_____

_____

_____

_____

_____

_____

_____

_____

_____

_____

_____

_____

_____

_____

_____

_____

_____

❄ ❄ ❄

Who was there Christmas Eve :

_____

_____

_____

_____

_____

_____

_____

_____

❄ ❄ ❄

Who was there Christmas Day :

_____

_____

_____

_____

_____

_____

_____

_____

❄ ❄ ❄

How we celebrated:

_____
_____
_____
_____
_____
_____
_____
_____
_____
_____
_____
_____
_____
_____
_____
_____
_____
_____
_____
_____

❄ ❄ ❄

What we ate at our Christmas dinner and who cooked what:

_____

_____

_____

_____

_____

_____

_____

_____

_____

_____

_____

_____

_____

_____

_____

_____

_____

_____

_____

_____

_____

_____

❄   ❄   ❄

This is what we wore:

❄ ❄ ❄

This is who came to visit:

❄ ❄ ❄

Memorable gifts that were exchanged and received:

❄ ❄ ❄

Favorite Christmastime
moment this year:

_____

_____

_____

_____

_____

_____

_____

_____

_____

_____

_____

_____

_____

_____

_____

_____

_____

❄   ❄   ❄

This is what we are thankful for this year:

❄ ❄ ❄

CHRISTMAS
THE
YEAR OF

_____

Where we celebrated the holidays:

_____

_____

❄ ❄ ❄

How we decorated our home:

———————————————————————————
———————————————————————————
———————————————————————————
———————————————————————————

❋   ❋   ❋

This was our new ornament/decoration:

———————————————————————————
———————————————————————————
———————————————————————————
———————————————————————————

❋   ❋   ❋

New holiday experience we had this year:

———————————————————————————
———————————————————————————
———————————————————————————
———————————————————————————

❋   ❋   ❋

Christmas parties we hosted or attended:

* * *

Favorite Christmas treats
we made or enjoyed together:

_____

_____

_____

_____

_____

_____

_____

_____

_____

_____

_____

_____

_____

_____

_____

_____

_____

❄ ❄ ❄

Who was there Christmas Eve:

❋ ❋ ❋

Who was there Christmas Day:

❋ ❋ ❋

How we celebrated:

❄ ❄ ❄

What we ate at our Christmas dinner and who cooked what:

_____

_____

_____

_____

_____

_____

_____

_____

_____

_____

_____

_____

_____

_____

_____

_____

_____

_____

❄ ❄ ❄

This is what we wore:

——————————————————

——————————————————

——————————————————

——————————————————

——————————————————

——————————————————

——————————————————

❄ ❄ ❄

This is who came to visit:

——————————————————

——————————————————

——————————————————

——————————————————

——————————————————

——————————————————

——————————————————

❄ ❄ ❄

Memorable gifts that were
exchanged and received:

_____
_____
_____
_____
_____
_____
_____
_____
_____
_____
_____
_____
_____
_____
_____
_____
_____
_____
_____

❄ ❄ ❄

Favorite Christmastime
moment this year:

_____

_____

_____

_____

_____

_____

_____

_____

_____

_____

_____

_____

_____

_____

_____

_____

_____

_____

❄ ❄ ❄

This is what we are thankful for this year:

❄ ❄ ❄

Favorite Christmas cards
we received this year:

Christmas

the

Year of

_____

Where we celebrated the holidays:

_____

_____

❄ ❄ ❄

How we decorated our home:

_____
_____
_____
_____

❄ ❄ ❄

This was our new ornament/decoration:

_____
_____
_____
_____

❄ ❄ ❄

New holiday experience we had this year:

_____
_____
_____
_____

❄ ❄ ❄

Christmas parties we hosted or attended:

_____
_____
_____
_____
_____
_____
_____
_____
_____
_____
_____
_____
_____
_____
_____
_____
_____
_____
_____
_____
_____
_____

❄ ❄ ❄

Favorite Christmas treats
we made or enjoyed together:

_____

_____

_____

_____

_____

_____

_____

_____

_____

_____

_____

_____

_____

_____

_____

_____

_____

_____

❄   ❄   ❄

Who was there Christmas Eve :

❄ ❄ ❄

Who was there Christmas Day :

❄ ❄ ❄

How we celebrated:

_____

_____

_____

_____

_____

_____

_____

_____

_____

_____

_____

_____

_____

_____

_____

_____

_____

_____

❄ ❄ ❄

What we ate at our Christmas dinner and who cooked what:

_____

_____

_____

_____

_____

_____

_____

_____

_____

_____

_____

_____

_____

_____

_____

_____

_____

_____

_____

_____

❄ ❄ ❄

This is what we wore:

_____

_____

_____

_____

_____

_____

_____

❄ ❄ ❄

This is who came to visit:

_____

_____

_____

_____

_____

_____

_____

❄ ❄ ❄

Memorable gifts that were exchanged and received:

_____

_____

_____

_____

_____

_____

_____

_____

_____

_____

_____

_____

_____

_____

_____

_____

_____

_____

❄ ❄ ❄

Favorite Christmastime
moment this year:

_____

_____

_____

_____

_____

_____

_____

_____

_____

_____

_____

_____

_____

_____

_____

_____

_____

_____

❄   ❄   ❄

This is what we are thankful for this year:

_____

_____

_____

_____

_____

_____

_____

_____

_____

_____

_____

_____

_____

_____

_____

_____

_____

_____

❄   ❄   ❄

Favorite Christmas cards
we received this year:

CHRISTMAS
THE
YEAR OF

_____

Where we celebrated the holidays:

_____

_____

❄   ❄   ❄

How we decorated our home:

_____
_____
_____
_____

❄ ❄ ❄

This was our new ornament/decoration:

_____
_____
_____
_____

❄ ❄ ❄

New holiday experience we had this year:

_____
_____
_____
_____

❄ ❄ ❄

Christmas parties we hosted or attended:

Favorite Christmas treats
we made or enjoyed together:

_____

_____

_____

_____

_____

_____

_____

_____

_____

_____

_____

_____

_____

_____

_____

_____

_____

_____

❄   ❄   ❄

Who was there Christmas Eve:

_____

_____

_____

_____

_____

_____

_____

_____

❄   ❄   ❄

Who was there Christmas Day:

_____

_____

_____

_____

_____

_____

_____

_____

❄   ❄   ❄

How we celebrated:

What we ate at our Christmas dinner and who cooked what:

_____

_____

_____

_____

_____

_____

_____

_____

_____

_____

_____

_____

_____

_____

_____

_____

_____

_____

❄   ❄   ❄

This is what we wore:

_____

_____

_____

_____

_____

_____

_____

❄   ❄   ❄

This is who came to visit:

_____

_____

_____

_____

_____

_____

_____

_____

❄   ❄   ❄

Memorable gifts that were
exchanged and received:

_____
_____
_____
_____
_____
_____
_____
_____
_____
_____
_____
_____
_____
_____
_____
_____
_____
_____

❊   ❊   ❊

Favorite Christmastime
moment this year:

This is what we are thankful for this year:

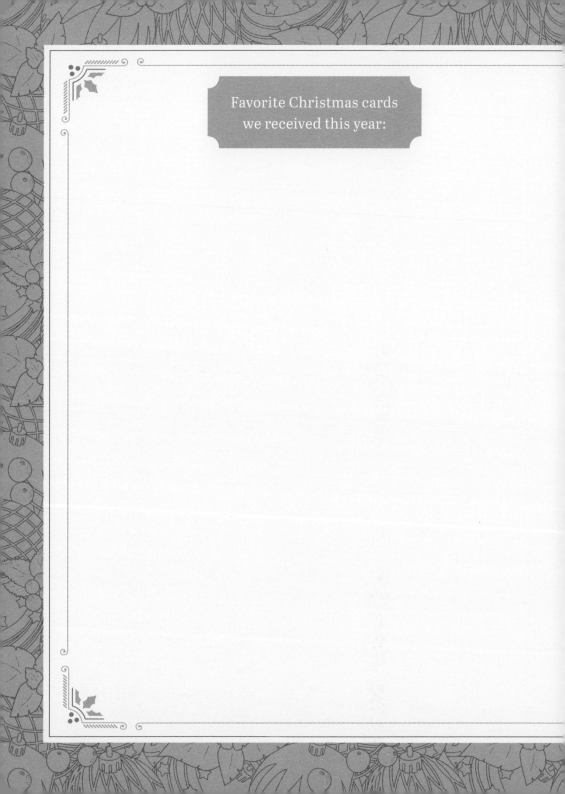

Favorite Christmas cards
we received this year:

A Collection of Favorite Family Recipes

Recipe Name:

From/Origin: Serves:

Prep Time/Total Time:

Ingredients:

❋ ❋ ❋

Directions:

_____

_____

_____

_____

_____

_____

_____

_____

_____

_____

_____

_____

_____

_____

_____

_____

_____

_____

_____

_____

_____

❄ ❄ ❄

Recipe Name:

_____

From/Origin: Serves:

_____   _____

Prep Time/Total Time:

_____

Ingredients:

_____

_____

_____

_____

_____

_____

_____

_____

_____

_____

_____

❄ ❄ ❄

Directions:

_____

_____

_____

_____

_____

_____

_____

_____

_____

_____

_____

_____

_____

_____

_____

_____

_____

_____

_____

❄ ❄ ❄

Recipe Name:

From/Origin: Serves:

Prep Time/Total Time:

Ingredients:

❄ ❄ ❄

Directions:

_____

_____

_____

_____

_____

_____

_____

_____

_____

_____

_____

_____

_____

_____

_____

_____

_____

_____

_____

_____

_____

_____

_____

❄ ❄ ❄

Recipe Name:

From/Origin:

Serves:

Prep Time/Total Time:

Ingredients:

✳ ✳ ✳

Directions:

_____
_____
_____
_____
_____
_____
_____
_____
_____
_____
_____
_____
_____
_____
_____
_____
_____
_____
_____
_____
_____

❄ ❄ ❄

Recipe Name:

From/Origin: Serves:

Prep Time/Total Time:

Ingredients:

❄   ❄   ❄

Directions:

❄ ❄ ❄

Recipe Name:

_____

From/Origin: Serves:

_____   _____

Prep Time/Total Time:

_____

Ingredients:

_____
_____
_____
_____
_____
_____
_____
_____
_____
_____

❄   ❄   ❄

Directions:

❄ ❄ ❄

Inspiring | Educating | Creating | Entertaining

Brimming with creative inspiration, how-to projects, and useful information to enrich your everyday life, quarto.com is a favorite destination for those pursuing their interests and passions.

© 2022 Quarto Publishing Group USA Inc.

This edition published in 2022 by Chartwell Books,
an imprint of The Quarto Group
142 West 36th Street, 4th Floor
New York, NY 10018 USA
T (212) 779-4972 F (212) 779-6058
www.Quarto.com

10 9 8 7 6 5 4 3 2 1

Chartwell titles are also available at discount for retail, wholesale, promotional, and bulk purchase. For details, contact the Special Sales Manager by email at specialsales@quarto.com or by mail at The Quarto Group, Attn: Special Sales Manager, 100 Cummings Center Suite 265D, Beverly, MA 01915, USA.

ISBN: 978-0-7858-4124-1

Publisher: Wendy Friedman
Editorial Director: Betina Cochran
Editor: Meredith Mennitt
Designer: Sue Boylan
Image credits: Shutterstock

Printed in China